SPARTANS

by Steven Otfinoski

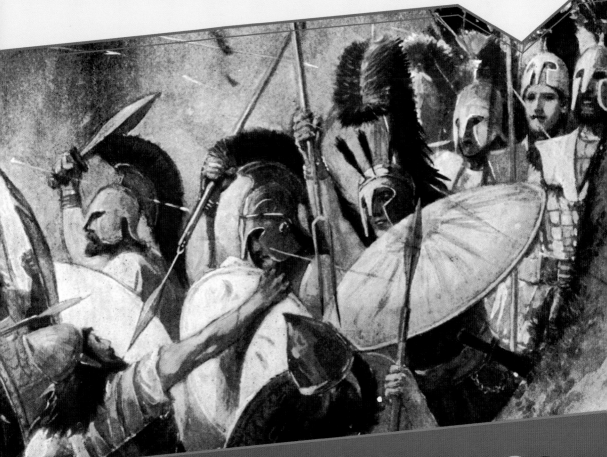

Content Consultant
Gary Eddy, Professor of English
Winona State University

CORE
LIBRARY

Published by ABDO Publishing Company, PO Box 398166, Minneapolis, MN 55439. Copyright © 2013 by Abdo Consulting Group, Inc. International copyrights reserved in all countries. No part of this book may be reproduced in any form without written permission from the publisher. The Core Library™ is a trademark and logo of ABDO Publishing Company.

Printed in the United States of America,
North Mankato, Minnesota
102012
012013

♻ THIS BOOK CONTAINS AT LEAST 10% RECYCLED MATERIALS.

Editor: Lauren Coss
Series Designer: Becky Daum

Library of Congress Cataloging-in-Publication Data
Otfinoski, Steven.
  Spartans / Steven Otfinoski.
    p. cm. -- (Great warriors)
Includes bibliographical references and index.
ISBN 978-1-61783-728-9
1. Sparta (Extinct city)--History, Military--Juvenile literature. 2. Soldiers--Greece--Sparta (Extinct city)--Juvenile literature. 1. Title.
938/.9--dc22

                                                        2012946372

Photo Credits: North Wind/North Wind Picture Archives, cover, 1, 12, 14, 16, 20, 22, 31; Time & Life Pictures/Getty Images, 4, 36; Red Line Editorial, 7; Hulton Archive/Getty Images, 9, 18; Time Life Pictures/Mansell/Time Life Pictures/Getty Images, 10; Dorling Kindersley, 25, 45; Dimitri Messinis/AP Images, 26; Thinkstock, 28, 38; Alexander S. Onassis Public Benefit Foundation/AP Images, 32; Gary Ombler/Dorling Kindersley, 35; Panos Karapanagiotis/Shutterstock Images, 40

CONTENTS

CHAPTER ONE

SPARTA VICTORIOUS

It was 405 BCE. And for once the Spartans seemed unwilling to fight. The Spartans and the Athenians had been caught up in the Peloponnesian War for 27 years. The Spartans were great warriors from the Greek city-state of Sparta. The Athenians came from Athens, another Greek city-state.

The Athenians were known for their mighty navy. Spartan soldiers were deadly on land.

The Peloponnesian War was really two wars separated by a six-year period of uneasy peace. It took its name from Peloponnesus, the lower peninsula of Greece where the city-state of Sparta was located. The conflict started in 431 BCE. That year the army of Thebes, an ally of Sparta, attacked Plataea, which was an ally of Athens. Both Athens and Sparta got involved in the fighting. Each city-state wanted to become the dominant power in Greece.

For four mornings in a row, the mighty fleet of Athenians had challenged the Spartan ships anchored nearby. The Athenians wanted a fight. But the Spartan commander, Lysander, refused each time. The Spartans weren't cowards. They had fiercely fought the Athenians during the long war. But their warriors were strongest on land. The Athenian navy, on the other hand, was strong on the seas.

The Athenians had 36,000 men on their ships. They appeared to be invincible.

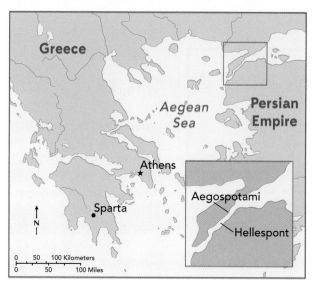

The Battle of Aegospotami
The Athenians were anchored at a beach at Aegospotami, a small harbor at a river mouth. From Aegospotami they sailed through a narrow passage called the Hellespont to reach the Spartans. This map shows the location of the Battle of Aegospotami. What information in the map helps you understand the battle better?

The Battle at Aegospotami

The Athenian general, Philocles, had an idea to trick the Spartans into fighting. He planned to head out of Aegospotami with a small fleet of just 30 ships. Then he would sail past the Spartan ships. He felt the Spartans wouldn't be able to resist attacking such a small fleet. They would be lured out of the harbor to chase the Athenians. The Spartans would be out on

Lysander

Lysander is remembered as the general who brought the great Peloponnesian War to an end. After the Athenian surrender, Lysander played an important role in controlling Athens. He led the Spartans in their new war against Thebes. Lysander was killed in 395 BCE while leading his army in an attack on the city of Haliartus, Greece.

the open water. Then the main Athenian fleet would attack the Spartan ships.

But Lysander was crafty too. When the small Athenian fleet sailed past, he and the Spartan ships attacked. But they were much quicker than Philocles expected. The Spartans cut off the Athenians' escape route. Philocles panicked. He sailed his small fleet back to Aegospotami. The Spartans followed. The larger Athenian fleet wasn't ready for an attack. Many of the ships were up on the beach. The ships' crews were relaxing on land. Lysander's ships drew close and landed on the beach. The shocked Athenian soldiers ran for their lives.

Lysander was a powerful military and political leader in ancient Sparta.

In a matter of hours, the Spartans captured 170 Athenian ships. Only ten ships escaped to the sea. Four thousand Athenian soldiers were taken prisoner and later executed. In the spring of 404 BCE, the Athenians surrendered to the Spartans. The Peloponnesian War was finally over.

Spartan soldiers were fierce fighters who were willing to die for their homeland.

Sparta on Top

The Spartans took warfare and patriotism to a new level. The Spartans valued order, honor, and military ability. The Spartan soldier was devoted to his fellow soldiers and the state. He spent most of his life training to fight. He would gladly die defending Sparta if necessary. This dedication created a unique society that turned out some of the greatest warriors ever known.

During the Peloponnesian War, the Spartans and the Athenians had many allies. The Argives of Argos, Greece, allied with the Athenians. In the first century BCE, the Greek historian Diodorus recorded an unusual showing of mercy by the Spartans:

> After the Spartans had routed the other parts of the army, killing many, they turned on the thousand elite Argives. . . . The King of the Spartans . . . would have killed them all . . . but he was not allowed to carry out his intention. For the Spartan Pharax, who was one of the advisers . . . commanded him to give an escape route to the elite troops and not by taking chances against men who had given up hope of living, to find out about the courage of men deserted by fortune. So the King was compelled by the orders he had recently received to allow their escape.

Source: Donald Kagan. The Peloponnesian War. New York: Viking, 2003. Print. 240.

Back It Up

The historian Diodorus uses evidence to support the idea that the Spartans could be merciful in battle. Write a few sentences describing the point Diodorus is making. Then write down two pieces of evidence Diodorus uses to make his point.

CHAPTER TWO

A WARRIOR PEOPLE

What became the mighty city-state of Sparta began as a tiny village on the Peloponnesian peninsula. The village was in an area of Greece known as Laconia. In the 1000s BCE, a group of Greeks called Dorians settled in the area. The Dorians came from northern Greece. They had little technology or government structure. But they were fierce fighters. They spread their culture

Ancient Sparta was located on a southern peninsula of Greece.

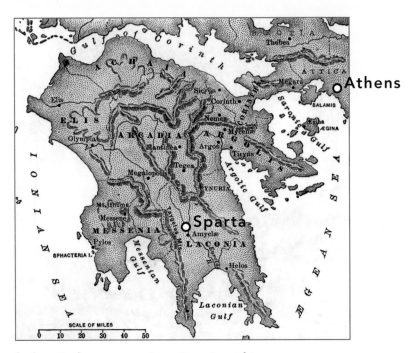

Map of the Peloponnesian Peninsula

This map shows the geography of the Peloponnesian peninsula. It includes the location of Sparta and Athens. Which of the two rival cities seems more isolated and protected from its enemies? Which one has better access to the sea? How does this compare to the information you learned about these two cities in the text?

into central Greece. The Spartans who descended from the Dorians kept their warlike nature. Within a few hundred years, the Spartans took control of all of Peloponnesus.

In the 500s BCE the Spartans founded the Peloponnesian League. The league was made up of neighboring city-states that Sparta dominated.

When the Spartans went to war with other Greek city-states, the members of the league were required to fight with Sparta. League members also benefited from the protection of Sparta.

The Persian War

In 481 BCE Persia (modern-day Iran) controlled a great empire to the east of Greece. Hoping to expand its empire, Persia launched an invasion of Greece. The Greek city-states joined together to fight off the invaders. The Persian king, Xerxes, led his army across the Hellespont and into Greece.

The Government of Sparta

Sparta was ruled by two kings. These kings also served as high priests and leaders in wartime. However they did not have total power. The kings had five advisers known as ephors. The main lawmaking body of the government was a senate. The senate was made up of the two kings and 28 elders. The senate limited the kings' powers. Some Spartan citizens could also vote on political decisions.

Three hundred Spartan warriors were able to hold off the Persian army at the pass of Thermopylae.

In August 480 BCE, 300 Spartan warriors made a stand against the Persians at the pass of Thermopylae. King Leonidas commanded the 300 Spartans. Their only mission was to hold back the Persians for as long as possible. The Persians greatly outnumbered the Spartans. The Spartans did not expect to win the fight. In the battle that followed, all 300 Spartans died fighting. But their sacrifice was not for nothing. By holding off the Persians, the Spartans gave the other Greeks valuable time to prepare to defend their territory.

The Immortal 300

Leonidas's men originally included nearly 7,000 Greek soldiers from city-states across Greece. A Greek traitor guided Xerxes through a mountain pass to surprise the Spartans from behind. Leonidas sent the main army to another location for safety. He and his group of 300 Spartans held their position at the Thermopylae pass. The pass was only 50 feet (15 m) wide. It sat between the mountains and the sea. The Persians killed Leonidas in the first battle. But the 300 fought on bravely without their leader.

Although King Leonidas died fighting the Persians, his courage made him a hero to the Spartans and their fellow Greeks.

A Greek Victory

A few weeks later, in September, the Athenians defeated the Persians in a great naval battle. Together Sparta and Athens had secured the Greek victory and driven out the Persians. However by 431 BCE, Sparta and Athens were fighting against each other in the Peloponnesian War.

Herodotus was a Greek historian who lived in the 400s BCE. In one of his books, Herodotus describes the brave stand the 300 Spartans took at Thermopylae:

> *The Spartan Dienekes is said to have proved himself the best man of all, the same who, as they report, uttered this saying before they engaged battle with the Medes: — being informed by one of the men of Trachis that when the Barbarians discharged their arrows they obscured the light of the sun by the multitude of the arrows, so great was the number of their host, he was not dismayed by this. . . . he said that their guest from Trachis brought them very good news, for if the Medes obscured the light of the sun, the battle against them would be in the shade and not in the sun.*

> *Source: Herodotus.* The History of Herodotus Volume Two. *Trans. G. C. Macaulay. Project Gutenberg, 2008. Web. Accessed 22 Aug. 2012.*

Consider Your Audience

Herodotus wrote this passage for an ancient Greek audience. How would you adapt it for a modern audience such as your friends? Write a blog post giving this same information to your new audience. How is your new approach different from the original text?

CHAPTER THREE

A SOLDIER'S LIFE

The Spartan government was very involved in its citizens' lives. When a male child was born, soldiers visited the baby's home. They decided if the boy was healthy enough to live. If the soldiers thought the baby appeared weak or in poor health, they would take the baby away from its family. Then they would abandon the baby in the wilderness

Spartan males were expected to work hard to become strong and able soldiers.

Spartan boys were taught to fight from a very young age.

to die. Only healthy, strong males were raised to adulthood in Sparta.

Soldiers in Training

Childhood for healthy Spartan boys ended at age seven. Then they were taken from their families and put into training centers. They were split into groups of 15. For the next 13 years, they received training in sports and warfare. They practiced gymnastics, running, and spear throwing.

The life of a Spartan boy was tough. The boys in training ate black broth and coarse wheat porridge. They wore simple, light clothing, regardless of the weather. They slept in common rooms on beds made of hard reeds. They learned to cope with pain and discomfort, including extreme temperatures. If a Spartan boy broke a rule, the older boys in his group beat him. Spartan youth were taught to be crafty as well as strong and courageous. They were encouraged to steal

The Boy and the Fox

Stories were important ways to convey lessons and wisdom to Spartan boys. One story was told countless times to inspire youths to live up to the tough demands placed on them by Spartan society. It was about a Spartan boy who caught a fox. Before he could kill and eat it, a group of soldiers came by. The boy did not want to be caught with the fox and punished, so he hid the fox under his shirt. As the soldiers talked to him, the fox began biting the boy's stomach. Although he was in pain, the boy did not reveal the fox. When the soldiers left, the boy collapsed. He later died of his stomach wounds. All who heard the story in ancient Sparta understood the moral: a Spartan shows no fear even at the cost of his life.

food when they could. But if they were caught, the boys were punished. The punishment was not for stealing. It was for being caught.

The boys worked hard. They knew soldiers were the highest class of Spartans. If a boy learned discipline and could fight well, he might earn the honor of becoming a soldier of Sparta.

Spartan Women

Spartan women were not raised to be soldiers. But they were still brought up to be physically strong and able. Like boys, girls were separated from their parents at age seven. They learned to read and write. Unlike other Greek girls, Spartan girls also learned how to play sports and fight with weapons. Spartan women had much more independence than other Greek women. Spartan men were often away from home fighting in wars. Many women ran family farms and businesses.

Life as a Soldier

At age 20, each young soldier-in-training had to undergo a tough physical test. If he failed the test, he would become a member of the middle class. Then he would train to be a tradesman

Being a Spartan soldier, left, was a dangerous job.

or a craftsman. If he passed the test, he became a full citizen and a Spartan soldier.

Each soldier was given a piece of land. Slaves called helots farmed the land for the soldier. The income from the farm supported the soldier. Young Spartan soldiers were expected to marry. But they didn't live with their wives. After marrying, a young soldier continued to live in soldiers' quarters. He would eat and sleep alongside his fellow soldiers.

Spartan soldiers were expected to be courageous. A statue of King Leonidas still stands in Greece, honoring his bravery.

At age 30, the soldier was allowed to live with his family. But he was expected to continue training. He would go to battle when Sparta became involved in a war. Now he was also allowed to vote in elections, attend annual meetings, and run for public office.

Later Life

If a soldier lived to age 60, he could retire from the service. He might be able to serve in the senate. But many Spartans never lived to retirement age. Many Spartan soldiers were killed in battle before reaching their sixtieth birthday.

Dying in battle was the highest honor a Spartan soldier could achieve. If a soldier died fighting, he was carried off the battlefield on his shield. He was given a funeral. His family mourned for him. But he would have died honorably. His shield and weapons would be passed on to a member of his family. It is said when a Spartan mother saw her son leave for war she would hand him his shield. Then she would tell him to bring back the shield or be brought back on top of it.

EXPLORE ONLINE

This chapter had a lot of information on the lives of Spartan soldiers. But there is much more to learn. Many Web sites offer great information. Visit the link below to explore more about Spartan families. How is the information on the Web site similar to the information in this chapter? What new facts and ideas does the Web site contain? What did you learn from this Web site?

History Wiz

www.historywiz.com/didyouknow/spartanfamily.htm

CHAPTER FOUR

WAR AND WEAPONS

Spartans went to war well prepared and well armed. The soldiers were groomed for battle from the time they were children. Spartan warriors' battle strategies and weapons made them some of the most feared warriors in Greece. They valued honor above all else. They were willing to defend their homeland to the death. In the 400s BCE,

Spartan soldiers were feared both for their battle techniques and their weapons.

at the height of Spartan power, there were more than 8,000 soldiers in the Spartan army.

The Phalanx

The Spartans fought in a pattern called a phalanx. Other ancient warriors had used the phalanx, but the Spartans perfected it. In a phalanx, soldiers were tightly grouped in a closed line. Each soldier held his shield in front of his body so it overlapped with the other shields in the line. Soldiers kept their spears extended in front of them. This way they were always ready to attack the enemy.

The width of the phalanx formation was always greater than its depth. By the 700s BCE, the average phalanx was eight men deep. The Spartans often changed the depth of their phalanxes. They wanted their enemies to never be sure how many soldiers they had.

Spartan armies, right, fought in a tight battle formation called a phalanx.

Battle Protection

In a phalanx, only the lower legs and the head were exposed to enemy attack. But Spartan soldiers still took care to protect their bodies. Soldiers wore armor plates called greaves that covered their shins. Most Spartan soldiers wore a breastplate made of bronze. Under his armor, a soldier wore a red tunic and a cloak. These items identified him as a Spartan.

Each Spartan soldier also wore a metal helmet to protect his head. The helmet covered the entire head. But it had openings in front for the eyes.

Spartan helmets featured a large crest to make the soldier wearing the helmet seem bigger.

Spartan helmets were made of sturdy bronze. Each one was decorated with a crest made of dyed horsehair. The crest made a soldier appear taller and scarier to the enemy.

A Hero's Shield

A shield was a Spartan soldier's prized possession and greatest protection. Spartan shields were round and made of wood. The shield was coated with a layer of bronze for extra protection and sturdiness. Soldiers strapped the shields to their left forearms.

The Spartan shield also served as a weapon. Spartan shields were very heavy and had a thin, sharp edge. A soldier could use it to knock an enemy down while he reached for another weapon. Spartans could also use their shields to beat an enemy to death if no other weapon was available.

Spears and Swords

A shield might have been a Spartan soldier's greatest protection, but his spear was his most important weapon. Spears were seven to nine feet (2.1 to 2.7 m) long. They had handles made of hard wood. The pointed spearhead was made from bronze or

A Legacy of Weapons

Weapons were among a Spartan's most prized possessions. A soldier who died in battle or retired from service often passed his weapons down to his son. Carrying a relative's weapons, especially a shield, into battle was a great honor. To lose or abandon a family shield or sword on the battlefield was seen as very cowardly. The sorry soldier who did so brought shame and disgrace on his entire family.

Strange Soldiers

After the Persian War, Athenians made great leaps in art, literature, philosophy, and science. Sparta played little part in this time of cultural advancements. Its focus remained on the art of war and little else. Other Greeks thought the Spartans' obsession with warfare was strange and uncivilized. Athenian artwork and pottery often showed Spartan soldiers fighting.

iron. The end was capped with a metal spike called a lizard killer. A soldier could also use the lizard killer as a weapon against his enemy if the spearhead was broken. In battle the Spartan soldier held his spear in one hand and his shield in the other.

A Spartan soldier's secondary weapon was his *xiphos* sword. The Spartan warrior used this sword when in close combat. A xiphos had a one- to two-foot-long (0.3- to 0.6-m long) blade. This length allowed the soldier to thrust his sword into an enemy soldier's body through an opening in his shield or armor.

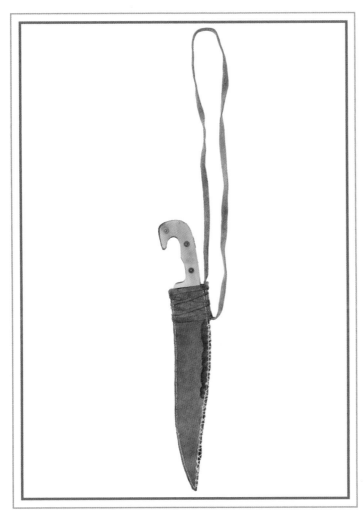

A Spartan used the shorter kopis for close-range fighting.

Spartans also carried a weapon called a *kopis*. A kopis had a thick, curved iron blade that could be used to stab an enemy. Soldiers used the kopis more like an axe than a sword. The Spartans' deadly power when using their weapons made them some of the most feared warriors of their time.

CHAPTER FIVE

A CHANGING GREECE

The Spartan warriors' way of life brought them great power in ancient Greece. But it also led to their destruction.

Sparta's conflict with Athens did not end with Sparta's victory in the Peloponnesian War in 404 BCE. The citizens of Athens and the other city-states of mainland Greece resented Sparta's newfound power.

Spartans were a powerful force in Greece in the 400s BCE. But their hold on the region would not last long.

Though Spartan soldiers had fallen from power, their legends lived on in stories and art.

In 378 BCE, Athens joined forces with Thebes. The two city-states went to war with Sparta.

The war could not have come at a worse time for Sparta. The helot slaves outnumbered Spartan citizens. They were native Greeks and tired of being under Spartan control. By the 300s, they staged rebellions involving many helots. Long years of war had worn down the Spartan army. It was able to put down helot uprisings. But the constant struggle took its toll on the army's numbers and energy. More and more soldiers were killed in battle or grew too old to fight. The Spartans were forced to hire foreign soldiers to fight for them.

A Weakened State

By 350 BCE, Sparta was just one of many Greek city-states that had been weakened by war. A new power was on the rise in the region: Macedonia to the north. By 339 BCE, Philip II of Macedonia had seized control of Sparta and the rest of Greece.

The Macedonian rule was short-lived. Romans in Italy had been working on their own empire. In the 100s BCE, Sparta became part of the Roman Empire. After a

A New Sparta

In 1834 Greeks founded a second Sparta on part of the ancient city's site. They called it New Sparta. During a Greek economic crisis in 2011, the people of New Sparta expressed their anger at the national government. The called themselves the Indignant Spartans. The group conducted a three-day march to Athens. Once there they peacefully protested against government policies.

The ruins of ancient Sparta lie on the same land as the modern city of Sparta, Greece.

long period of decline, a group of Germanic invaders known as Visigoths destroyed the city of Sparta in 396 CE.

Sparta's Long Legacy

Spartan warriors were men of action. They were devoted to their homeland and willing to die in its defense. The Spartan society created some of the bravest and most talented fighters of the ancient world. The Spartan period of supremacy had lasted a little more than 30 years. But Sparta continues to be remembered around the world.

In popular culture the Spartans are the subjects of novels, comic books, video games, and more. Several movies have been made about the Spartans. One film about the 300 Spartans who fought at the Battle of Thermopylae was a box-office hit in 2006. Ancient Spartans have been gone for more than 2,000 years. But they continue to fascinate and inspire cultures and societies around the world.

FURTHER EVIDENCE

This chapter focused on ancient Sparta's downfall and its legacy. What are the chapter's main points? What details from the chapter support those key ideas? Visit the Web site below. Find a quote that adds a new piece of evidence to the chapter's main points. How does this new information change your understanding of the Spartans?

History for Kids

www.historyforkids.org/learn/greeks/government/spartans.htm

IMPORTANT DATES AND BATTLES

500s BCE

Sparta establishes the Peloponnesian League, a group of city-states Sparta dominates.

481 BCE

Persian king Xerxes launches an invasion of Greece, beginning the Persian War.

480 BCE

King Leonidas leads 300 Spartan soldiers in defending the pass of Thermopylae from the invading Persians.

404 BCE

The Peloponnesian War ends.

378 BCE

Thebes and Athens join forces to go to war against Sparta.

339 BCE

King Philip II of Macedonia takes control of Sparta and the rest of Greece.

480 BCE

The Athenian naval fleet defeats the Persians decisively at sea with assistance on land from the Spartan army.

431 BCE

The Peloponnesian War between Athens and Sparta begins.

405 BCE

The Spartan fleet captures the Athenian fleet in a stunning victory even though the Athenian ships outnumber Spartan ships.

100s BCE

Sparta becomes part of the Roman Empire.

396 CE

Visigoths destroy Sparta.

1834 CE

Greeks build the town of New Sparta on the site of ancient Sparta.

Why Do I Care?

Spartan soldiers may have lived long ago, but your life may not be as different from a Spartan's as you think. Have you ever worked hard to achieve something special? Have you ever been away from your family at a summer camp or another special activity group? What was it like? Write down two or three ways that the Spartans and their way of life connect to your life.

Take a Stand

This book focuses on the Spartan way of life. It also gives some information about how the Athenians lived. Which of these Greek societies do you think had a more lasting impact on society? Why? Write a short essay explaining your opinion. Include your reasons for your opinion and give some facts and details to support those reasons.

Another View

Find another source about the Spartans of ancient Greece. Write a short essay comparing and contrasting its point of view with the view of this book's author. Answer these questions as you write: What is the point of view of each author? How are they similar and why? How are they different and why?

You Are There

Imagine that you are one of the 300 Spartans at the Battle of Thermopylae. What defensive precautions do you take? What are your feelings about the coming fight? How do you think your fellow soldiers feel?

GLOSSARY

city-state
a self-governing state made of a city and its surrounding territory

crest
an ornament or decoration on a soldier's helmet

elder
a lawmaker in Sparta

ephors
advisers to the kings of Sparta

fleet
a group of ships sailing together, often into battle

greaves
armor plates that protect a soldier's shins in battle

helots
a class of native Greek people in Sparta with few rights who served as workers on the land

invincible
unbeatable

kopis
a small sword with a thick, curved blade

patriotism
loyalty to one's country

peninsula
a region connected to the mainland by a strip of land

phalanx
a fighting formation where soldiers are grouped in a tight unit in a closed line

xiphos
a short Spartan sword

LEARN MORE

Books

Cobblestone Publishers. *If I Were A Kid in Ancient Greece*. Peterborough, NH: Cricket Books, 2006.

Park, Louise. *The Spartan Hoplites*. Tarrytown, NY: Marshall Cavendish, 2009.

Pearson, Anne. *Ancient Greece*. New York: DK Children, 2007.

Web Links

To learn more about Spartan warriors, visit ABDO Publishing Company online at **www.abdopublishing.com.** Web sites about Spartan warriors are featured on our Book Links page. These links are routinely monitored and updated to provide the most current information available.

Visit **www.mycorelibrary.com** for free additional tools for teachers and students.

INDEX

ABOUT THE AUTHOR

Steven Otfinoski has written more than 150 books for young adults. He is also a teacher, playwright, and novelist. Otfinoski lives in Connecticut with his wife, their daughter, and two dogs.